DREAM BIG!

I DARE YOU . . .

BETTER YET...

I DOUBLE DARE YOU!!

ROGER PALMIERI

DREAM BIG I DARE YOU
BETTER YET... I DOUBLE DARE YOU!!

Published in New York, New York, by Morgan James Publishing. Morgan James and The Entrepreneurial Publisher are trademarks of Morgan James, LLC. www.MorganJamesPublishing.com.

The Morgan James Speakers Group can bring authors to your live event. For more information or to book an event visit The Morgan James Speakers Group at www.TheMorganJamesSpeakersGroup.com.

BitLit
FOR ALL THE BOOKS YOU OWN

FREE eBook edition for your existing eReader with purchase

PRINT NAME ABOVE

For more information, instructions, restrictions, and to register your copy, go to www.bitlit.ca/readers/register or use your QR Reader to scan the barcode:

ISBN 9781614489269   paperback
ISBN 9781630470005   eBook

Cover Design Concept by:
Carolyn Palmieri

Interior Design by:
Stephanie Anderson

Proud Supporter
"Dream Paws For Wounded Warriors"

Service Dogs For Our Military Heroes –

The mission of The Palmieri Group is to improve the quality of life for our service members that have been severely injured mentally, physically and emotionally by use of a service dog trained to assist them with their specific needs.

The Palmieri Group donates a portion of all book sales for the training of these service dogs.

In loving memory of my best friend, Dave, my fellow Marine, who while serving together, gave his life for his country in Vietnam. –Jan. 24, 1968

"Promise Made – Promise Kept"

Dedicated to the Dreamers

I dedicate this book to the human spirit of determination that is alive, well and expanding inside each of you. I encourage you to DREAM ... and DREAM BIG! I DARE YOU! ... for it is your dreams and the path you walk as you reach for them that will truly make a difference in your world, and the worlds of all those whose lives you touch.

To Carolyn,
the Center of my Universe

You inspired me, believed in me,
    and encouraged me to do greater things.
You believed in me when no one else
    did and when I forgot to.
Your love, friendship, wisdom, and
    strength continue to inspire me to
    DREAM BIG.
Thank you for always being my
    number one fan and I look forward to
    spending the rest of our lives together.

CONTENTS

INTRODUCTION

FOR THE PAST 35 YEARS, I have been teaching and training teams, groups and individuals to reach for and create success and self-fulfillment. As I have stood in front of training rooms, or taken my seat as facilitator in circles of motivated individuals, I am consistently amazed at the determination that lives in the human spirit. Sometimes that determination is easy to spot through the look in someone's eyes or the uprightness of their posture. Sometimes it is loudly stated as someone declares that they deserve what they want. And sometimes it takes a little prodding before the drive to achieve peeks its head out from under a hesitancy created by a recent failure or set-back.

But, no matter what, it is always there.

What is it about the human spirit that keeps us pushing forward? Where does the drive to be more, better, broader, more useful and more successful come from?

In my experience, the common denominator is this: there is an "intangible something" that excites, engages, and inspires each of us, pulling us forward toward **being** more, **doing** more and **having** more. Most people refer to this inspiration as **THEIR DREAM!**

Time and time again I have witnessed the positive changes and miracles that show up in people's lives when they commit to living their dreams. THERE ARE NO EXCEPTIONS! If you Dream it and you GO FOR IT—YOU WILL HAVE IT !!!!

Why do some people become highly successful and make the cover of TIME magazine—and others don't?

The difference is the specifics and expansiveness of their DREAM and the depth of the PASSION that fuels that person to GO FOR IT.

Period. Everyone is equal when it comes to the ability to bring their dreams into reality. The only difference is the actual DREAM itself and what a person is willing to do to make it happen.

Since you have a dream anyway—and I assume since you are reading this that you are feeling that your dream can be bigger than it is right now.....why not just DREAM BIG!

That's right. DREAM BIG!

Don't rationalize it. Don't try to figure out how you will make it real. Don't wonder if you can really have what you want. JUST DREAM BIG!

I believe so much in your ability to have your dreams come true that I DARE YOU to DREAM BIG!

In fact, I DOUBLE DARE YOU.

ALL YOU HAVE TO DO RIGHT NOW IS TAKE THE DARE ... AND YOU ARE ON YOUR WAY.

66 May all of your
dreams become reality
and all of your efforts
become magnificent
achievements. 99

ROGER PALMIERI

Stand Tall

There is no one else exactly like you. You are one of a kind.

FROM MY PERSONAL JOURNAL

YOU ARE IT

THERE IS ONLY ONE YOU in all space and time.

Think about that for a minute....

There are just over 7 billion people on this planet.

AND THERE IS ONLY ONE YOU.

No one else has your exact set of experiences, talents, insights, desires, fingerprints . . . or dreams.

Overwhelming, isn't it? And also, very interesting.

Why would every human on this planet be different from all other humans?

Here's my theory. In the overall plan of the evolution of mankind and life on planet Earth, every single one of us is needed. Each of us is here for a purpose. We all play a unique part in life (even if we don't know what it is.)

The part we are here to play tries time and time again to get our attention through our DREAMS. Not those blurry visions that come to us as we sleep. But those that seem to squiggle around inside of us and keep showing up when we are daydreaming. The visions that make us feel warm and fuzzy inside or fired up and inspired. The ideas that when they pop up, we say, "Wouldn't that be so cool!"

Your dreams are incessantly tapping you on the shoulder, nudging you spiritually and emotionally. Your inner voice is encouraging you to live as you know, deep down inside, that you can. It is saying, "Remember I am here. I am always right here inside of you. I want to come true for you! It's our time!"

Those feelings are telling you there is something inside of you, calling out to you, asking you to GO FOR IT! Go Ahead. Listen.

IT IS YOUR RESPONSIBILITY—AND YOUR HONOR—TO FOLLOW YOUR INNER GUIDANCE AND GO FOR YOUR DREAMS.

AND IT IS YOUR PATH TO SUCCESS AND HAPPINESS.

I bet you are feeling a bit challenged right now. I hope so.

The spark inside you deserves your attention. And the world deserves—and needs—for you to go for your dream.

Keep reading and let me help you turn that spark into a flame.

You are not defined by what you are given at birth. Success and happiness are not genetically transmitted attributes. Yes, your genes may define certain physical attributes like hair and eye color, height and general stature. But genetics do not place limits on the human spirit, the power of your will, or your ability to achieve. And those are the priceless tools you use to design your life. You will accomplish great things if you have the right environment that nurtures your dreams—not the right genes.

At eight years old, Derek Jeter decided he wanted to play short stop for the New York Yankees. In his biography, *The Life You Imagine*, he tells how he thought about it, dreamt about it and visualized it.

When he announced his intention to his parents, they told him he could do it, but he would have to work hard at it for a very long time.

Jeter's parents did not give him the "why nots." They did not tell him he was too skinny and not very big. They did not tell him that no one in his bloodline has ever played professional sports. Instead, they nurtured his dream, added fuel to his desire, and gave him a simple formula to make it happen—work hard.

And that is just what he did. When he was a senior in high school, Jeter weighed in at 155 pounds. Not exactly the size you would expect to make it in the major league. Yet he worked and worked and worked. At 18, ten years after he began working to live his dream, Jeter was drafted by his dream team. Two years later, he made it to the big show. And 18 years later, he is playing for the same team.

And he is still working hard. Now, at 38, he is hitting harder and running faster than he has in years. Because his burning desire was nurtured, he is still living his dream.

In his book, *The Biology of Belief,* cellular biologist Bruce Lipton blows the "you are your genes" theory to smithereens. In his research, he uncovered something interesting.

Your genes are activated or made dormant by your environment.

Through the research of Dr. Lipton, stunning new discoveries have been made about the interaction between your mind and body and the processes by which cells receive information. It shows that genes and DNA do not control our biology; that instead DNA is controlled by signals from outside the cell, including the energetic messages emanating from our thoughts.

You have the genes to succeed. All you need is people and environments that nurture you, train you, teach you and believe in you, and your talent will fully express itself.

Alice in Wonderland

"Would you tell me, please, which way I ought to go from here?" asked Alice

"That depends a good deal on where you want to get to," said the cat.

"I don't much care where," said Alice

"Then it doesn't matter which way you go," said the cat.

Dreams fuel revolutions and evolution. They change the world and create worlds we never thought possible. Everything that has ever been created began as a spark of inspiration. If something has not been dreamed about—it will not come about.

DREAM BIG

DO YOU CARE HOW your life turns out? I ask every person who I coach, teach, nurture or present this question. Why? Because if you care, even the tiniest bit, you are a dreamer. If you have someplace you want to get in life, something you want to experience, something you want to achieve, you are already exercising your power to dream. By knowing you want to get somewhere that is not "HERE," you are embarking on the path of having those dreams come true.

There is another part to the equation: you can't get THERE unless you know where THERE is.

How well do you know what you want? Can you see it, feel it, taste it? Is your dream mushy or full of muscle? If someone asks you what you want, can you give them a ten word answer that makes you smile and stand a little taller—and makes them say "Wow?"

Once you can state your dream that clearly, and with certainty and enthusiasm, you will find that all sorts of support, from expected and unexpected places, will begin to show up in your life! You will naturally begin to draw to you what you need to make your dream real.

In fact, once you discover and define your dream, put it front and center in your life, engage it fully and consistently take inspired action that supports your dream—YOU become unstoppable and your dream will become REAL.

One more thing. It takes the same amount of energy to make every dream come true. That's right. No matter what size your dream is, it will take the same amount of energy, focus, and action to make it real. The difference size makes is in the duration of the energy, focus, and action you will put in to keep that particular dream going.

Remember Derek Jeter? He had a BIG DREAM, a really BIG DREAM. He made it REAL. Today he is still applying his energy and focus, and taking action (working hard) to keep the dream alive. Now, if his dream had been to play baseball while in high school (let's call it his "little dream"), **he would have had to apply the same amount of hard work to make his little dream real.** But once he reached his little dream goal (playing baseball in high school), *he was already in motion and had built confidence. That momentum and confidence propelled him forward to his BIG DREAM* (playing for the Yankees in the majors).

This is a vitally important point.

It takes as much energy, focus and action to manifest a little dream as it does to manifest a BIG DREAM. The difference is how long you maintain the energy, focus and actions toward that particular dream.

Since you are going to make your dream come true, you might as well DREAM BIG!

Ultimately, your BIG Dream becomes your life fulfilling task. The little dreams you create along the way become your BIG DREAM "to do" list. You get to have all your little dreams come true on the way to your BIG DREAM. How cool is that?

So, Dream Big! I DARE YOU!

Tell me my dreams are
unrealistic and I will
tell you your dreams
are not big enough.

FROM MY PERSONAL JOURNAL

LET'S MAKE IT REAL :

Write your dream in the blank area below. Don't think about it. Close your eyes. Get a picture of it. And just write!

Now, get a bigger piece of paper and fill it up.......write everything that comes into your head, or thoughts, or mind's eye. Just write! Do not edit. This is not a test. This is you listening and allowing your dream to talk to you!

EXERCISE TIP #1: If your dream seems manageable—it is not BIG enough. Little dreams are manageable. Big Dreams are marvelous. Go ahead, stretch. Tell the truth. What do you really, really, really WANT?

EXERCISE TIP #2: When you were 5 years old, what did you want to be when you grew up?

Go For It! This is not just an exercise. This is your life!

★
KEEP WRITING YOUR
BIG DREAM HERE

Now write a clear statement of
your BIG DREAM in this box.

Keep it to ten words or less

MY BIG DREAM IS TO ....

_____

_____

_____

_____

_____

_____

_____

_____

Now, read your BIG DREAM statement, take a deep breath and answer the following questions:

What does your BIG DREAM **taste** like?

_____

_____

_____

What does your BIG DREAM **smell** like?

_____

_____

_____

What does your BIG DREAM **sound** like?

_____

_____

_____

What does your BIG DREAM **feel** like?

_____

_____

_____

What does your BIG DREAM **look** like?

_____

_____

_____

What is your **favorite thing** about your BIG DREAM?

_____

_____

_____

Now you have concrete clues that will let you know when you are on track as you take actions to bring your BIG DREAM into reality.

GREAT JOB !!!!!

The person who gets the farthest
is generally the one who is willing
to do and dare. The sure-thing
boat never gets far from shore.

DALE CARNEGIE

I D.A.R.E. YOU !!!

L ET'S BE CLEAR!
I am officially issuing you a DARE!
I am DARING you to DREAM BIG!

Did you just feel your adrenaline kick in? Did the hairs on the back of your neck stand up? Did your breathing become shallower? That's what happens when you have been challenged.

Feels pretty good, doesn't it? Don't you feel more alive than you did a minute ago? Well, technically, you are more alive. Your autonomic response systems—your heart rate, breathing, brain activity, just increased several notches. You are more alert. Things around you are clearer and more distinct. You awareness is heightened. Every one of your senses is on high alert. Right now you could actually run a little faster than you usually do.

Or you can stand your ground and channel that expanded energy into making things happen. That is the choice you face right now. Take your stand and make things happen. Or run.

Wait a minute. Did a little voice inside of you just pipe up, telling you that dreaming big is selfish, greedy, egotistical and sure to set you on a path of self-destruction ... or disappointment? Is it telling you that dreams come true for other people, but not for you? Is it telling you that you do not deserve to have what you want?

If you heard that little voice, did you go from feeling hopeful and fired up to doubtful or afraid? One minute ago you were feeling more alive. And now you might be feeling guilty and defeated.

We humans are complex beings. We have many layers of response systems—both instinctual and learned—that face off inside of us every day. We often feel we are in a tug of war, playing a push-pull game between being all that we can be, and staying small so that we can stay safe in our comfort zone.

Hopefully, one day someone or something comes along and because of their or its influence, something inside of us shifts. We plant our feet on the ground and find the strength to pull our desire to have our dreams across the line and it becomes a bigger part of our life than our fears and doubts.

I want TODAY to be that day for YOU. Just think. You have waited a long time. And TODAY can be THAT DAY for you.

That is why I am DARING you.

By its most basic definition, a DARE is *a challenge that allows you to access your courage.* That is what a dare "is." And, you are going to need courage to make your dreams come true. More important than what a DARE is, is what a DARE "does."

A DARE (D.A.R.E.) presents you with an *opportunity.* It puts whatever you are being dared to do in your face, in an emotional way. It forces you to determine what matters most to you. It forces a choice, to either take it or leave it. When you make that choice, you know where you stand in relation to the topic of the dare.

By going through the process of evaluating a DARE, whether that takes a second or a month, you find out where you are willing to take a stand. This is very valuable information that you can use as you move forward along your life path.

In this regard, a DARE is a very important tool—a technology—that allows you to know yourself better.

When I DARE you to DREAM BIG, I am really asking you a very important question:

Are you willing to:

DO
what it takes to

ALIGN
your

REALITY
with your

EXPECTATIONS

That's what the DREAM BIG Dare is all about. It is a way for you to (1) find out how you and your personal beliefs and philosophy of life line up with your dream and (2) gauge your level of desire to DO something about it. It is an exploration that allows you to assess your willingness in this moment. **This is good news, very good news.** Why?

Because **you** have the power to change your focus and your willingness at any time.

So let's use the DREAM BIG DARE to its full advantage, by looking at the individual exploration areas behind a DARE.

D₀... Align... Reality... Expectations

When someone turns their dream into reality, we call them a hero. Heroes don't start out that way. They become heroes by how they respond to the hardships they encounter in life.

Helen Keller became deaf, dumb and blind shortly after birth. Despite this greatest misfortune, she has written her name indelibly in the pages of history as one who overcame adversity to become great. Her entire life has served as evidence that no one is ever defeated until defeat has been accepted as reality.

Beethoven was deaf. **Milton** was blind. But their names will last as long as time endures, because they dreamed and translated their dreams into organized thoughts that became timeless masterpieces.

Dr. Martin Luther King, Jr. had a dream. That dream defined his entire life, inspired thousands and began a revolution that changed the world for the better.

Jim Carrey was completely broke and living in his car when he was just starting out in Hollywood. He decided to write himself a check for $10 million in 1985. He dated it Thanksgiving 1995 and noted at the bottom that it was "for acting services rendered." He carried that check with him in his wallet and looked at it every day. Six months before Thanksgiving 1995, he was paid $10 million for his work in the film Dumb and Dumber.

Nick Vajicic was unexplainably born without arms and legs, and life was an uphill battle. Life was so hard for him, he attempted suicide several times before he reached his teenage years. With the support of his loving, supportive family, and a strong Christian faith, he slowly began to focus on his abilities rather than his disabilities. One day, a janitor at his high school suggested that he begin speaking to others about his faith and overcoming adversity. He listened. He was inspired. He had found his purpose. By the age of 25, Nick had traveled to over 44 countries and given 2,000 motivational speeches. At 19, he started his first company, Attitude is Altitude. In 2007, he moved from his birthplace, Australia, to Los Angeles where he is CEO of the non-profit company, Life Without Limbs. Today he inspires millions to go for their dreams and never give up, no matter what.

Bethany Hamilton was born to be a surfer. At eight years old, she entered her first surfing competition—and won. She could not imagine doing anything else. She was full steam ahead to live her dream— being a professional surfer. At 13, Bethany was attacked by a tiger shark and lost her left arm. Even with this devastatingly traumatic event,

Bethany did not hesitate. One month after the event, Bethany was back in the water. Two months later, she entered her first competition. She placed fifth. One-year later, 14 year old Bethany won her first National Title. In 2007, three years after her injury, at the age of 17, Bethany turned pro. She continues to share her experiences through her autobiography, *Soul Surfer*, that has also been made into a major motion picture. She recently launched her own foundation, Friends of Bethany, dedicated to supporting shark attack survivors and traumatic amputees, and to inspiring others.

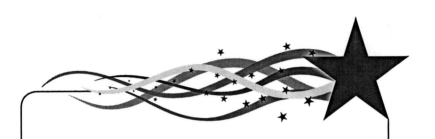

When I was a boy, I always saw myself as a hero in comic books and in movies. I grew up believing that dream.

ELVIS PRESLEY

Courage to follow your dreams is the first step to fulfilling your destiny.

FROM MY PERSONAL JOURNAL

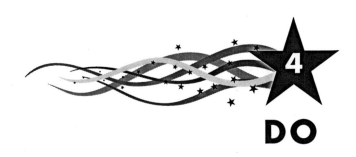

Do... **A**lign... **R**eality... **E**xpectations

WHAT AMOUNT OF ENERGY and resources are you willing to put toward your dream? What are you willing to give, and give up, in order to make your dreams a priority.... and a reality?

When we have a burning desire to create something, we are naturally inspired to DO what it takes to have what we desire. Action follows passion! You can gauge the level of your passion by looking at what you are willing to give to your dream. Your answer gives you insight into the level of emotional investment you have in your dream.

So, read the following questions and write down your answer below. There are no right or wrong answers. Just tell the truth. Remember, we are using these questions as an exploration.

What amount of energy and resources are you willing to put toward your dream?

_____

_____

_____

What are you willing to give, and give up, in order to make your dream a priority.... and a reality?

_____

_____

_____

Now, if your answer above is anything other than "Whatever it takes," we know there is something about how you have stated your dream that is not quite jiving for you. You need to experiment with stating your dream in a way that engages you totally and deeply at an emotional level. Words have power. Words create emotional responses. **For a dream to become real, it must be stated in words that sing to your heart and soul—not just to your head.**

With the right combination of words that express your true passion, purpose and desires, your answer to the DO question will be "Whatever it takes."

Play with the wording of your dream until it feels absolutely right. Now write it in the box on the following page.

My BIG DREAM is:

Well done. This is your dream statement for now. As with all things, your dream statement will change from time to time. (As you read this book it will get bigger and bigger!) Be flexible. Hold steadfast to your dream, but don't become too attached to how it is stated right now. That statement will expand as you do.

Now, let's take one more look at the DO questions at the beginning of this chapter. How many times do you see the word "do" in those sentences?

Zero. That's right. Zero. The question does not ask *what you are going to do*. It asks you *what you are willing to give*.

What you are willing to give is much more important to having your dream than what you are willing to do.

How can that be? When you commit to going for your BIG DREAM, you may only be able to determine your first inspired action step. If you are lucky, you may also be able to define steps two and three. *This is a good thing. It is not necessary to have the path to our dream all figured out. If we do, we miss miracles, unforeseen opportunities and just plain magic that show up along the way.*

Keep your focus on what you are willing to give rather than what you are going to do. And trust that through inspiration, what you are to do next will continue to reveal itself.

LET'S MAKE IT REAL

You will walk the path to your BIG DREAM one step at a time.

What is your first inspired step? Write what immediately comes to mind in the space below.

My first inspired step toward my BIG DREAM is:

_____

_____

_____

_____

_____

_____

_____

Excellent! You now have something that you can give your dream **right now** that will bring it closer to you.

Did you notice I said **right now?**

This is your BIG DREAM! Why wait?

When you are inspired to do something or give something to your dream, take that inspired step NOW!

Make a commitment and hold yourself to it. It is easier than you think. Just complete the sentence below.

I, _____ (your name),

take my first inspired step

toward my BIG DREAM on

_____ (today's date).

X _____

(sign your name)

**Now, take that step. Stop
reading and DO IT!**

Well done. When you act on the inspirations that come your way, more and more of them will show up in your life. Just stay focused on your BIG DREAM and pay attention.

**Right now, you are one step closer to
your BIG DREAM being realized!**

BRAVO!

The Butterfly Effect

In 1961, while working as an assistant in the department of meteorology at the Massachusetts Institute of Technology, Edward Lorenz created an early computer model to simulate weather. One day he changed one of a dozen numbers representing atmospheric conditions from .506127 to .506. This miniscule alteration utterly transformed his long term forecast.

He detailed his findings in a paper published in 1972, entitled ***"Predictability: Does the Flap of a Butterfly's Wings in Brazil Set off a Tornado in Texas?"*** Since that time, the Butterfly Effect, as his theory is commonly called, has been studied in all areas of science.

How does this apply to you?

Every decision you make—no matter how small—will alter the course of your life. All things are connected, often in ways you cannot imagine. By changing one thing, you change everything.

Details matter. *Overlooking one opportunity, one decision or one chance to make a difference creates far-reaching ripples into your future.*

You have no way of knowing or determining how even the seemingly insignificant actions you take will impact the world. But, because of the Butterfly

Effect, we know that somehow, they will. That impact can be positive or negative, depending on your intent and the action you take.

Hold a positive intention and take one small positive action every day. Then you can fall asleep every night knowing that this day you have made a positive difference in the world.

A sure way to have sweet dreams.

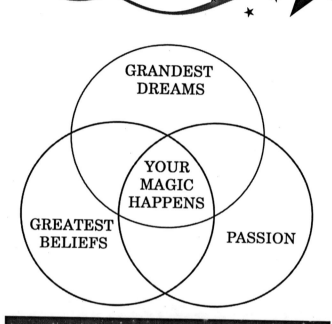

At the intersection of your grandest dreams and greatest beliefs, fueled by your relentless passion, is where your magic happens.

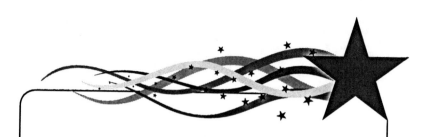

 So you want a

guarantee that your

Big Dream will be realized?

Well, here it is:

Follow your Passion

with Purposeful

Action ... I Dare You!!

ROGER PALMIERI

Just as your car runs more smoothly
and requires less energy to go faster
and farther when the wheels are in
perfect alignment, you perform better
when your thoughts, feelings, emotions,
goals, and values are in balance.

BRIAN TRACY

ALIGN

D_{o...} **A**lign... R_{eality...} E_{xpectations}

ARE ALL YOUR SYSTEMS and resources working together in harmony? Do you feel the magic in the air?

When was the last time you looked up from what you were doing and noticed hours have gone by? Think back to a moment when you were engaged in something special and meaningful and time seemed to stop. Is there something you do on a regular basis that is effortless? In fact, when someone asks you how you do that thing, you cannot even really tell them.

This is how people often describe "being in the flow." What an amazing experience when things seem to line up and happen with ease, joy and minimal effort. In the D.A.R.E. exploration, this is what ALIGN is all about.

What do **you** have to do with things lining up? Just about everything.

You are the vehicle through which your dream is going to express. It is your mind, your body, your emotions, your beliefs, and your will that provide the environment and energy through which your BIG DREAM will become real. When all these dream building blocks are lined up in a row, **you are unstoppable**.

Going for your dreams requires clarity and focus. Otherwise, the path to your dreams will be shaky and a struggle.

When you are strong, centered and focused in body, spirit and mind, fueled by your dream, and emotionally engaged in the journey, your path is unobstructed. Everything flows. MAGIC shows up.

Let's leave that ideal world for a moment. We are not always going to have all of our dream building blocks lined up in a neat, balanced row. That is not how life is, even for people who have unlimited resources and no worries. Some days are better than others. We all have highs and lows, challenges and victories, moments of clarity and spells of uncertainty. That is part of being human.

Once we accept this as part of the human experience, rather than being unnerved and detoured when things seem to go off balance, we can take this in stride. Instead of thinking all is lost, we will know this is just a temporary state. Then, we can focus on finding out which dream building block has moved out of balance, upsetting our alignment. We can give that area of our life some special attention and get "back in the flow."

We cannot avoid the ups and downs, the delays and detours of life. But we can certainly minimize them by knowing we have the ability to take care of ourselves, enhance our internal alignment, and then move forward more effortlessly.

Let's Make it Real

We all have activities we do easily and effortlessly, bringing us joy and moving us back into alignment with our "flow."

Some of us meditate, read, or take an exercise class. Others journal, walk their dog, play piano or doodle.

What do you do when you are feeling out of sync and want to get back in the flow?

Write five activities on the following page that bring you back toward your center of power.

★

1

2

3

4

5

This is your "go to" list when you are feeling stuck, uncertain, frustrated, or discouraged. When inspiration seems to be hiding out, pick a flow activity from your list and do it. Get out of your head and change your energetic state.

**Then pay attention and
see what shows up.**

Once upon a time there was a baby elephant. He was born to two very big elephants that worked in a circus. Shortly after he was born, he was tethered by a stout chain to a post, when he wasn't rehearsing his part in the circus. Over time, the elephant grew, and, even though he was getting bigger and bigger, the chain was replaced by smaller and smaller chains. The elephant did not realize he was much stronger than the small chain that was holding him to the small stake. So, he stayed put.

How could this beautiful, magnificent animal just stand there and make no attempt to get away?

It's a matter of conditioning. When the elephant was a baby, the strong chain was enough to hold him. As he grew, he was conditioned to believe he could not break away. He believed the smaller chain could still hold him. He never even tried to break free. He could have at any time broken his bonds, and freed himself. Because he believed he couldn't, he was stuck right where he was.

What beliefs (chains) have you been conditioned to **and** accept as your reality?

_____

_____

_____

_____

_____

_____

_____

_____

_____

_____

Dreams are our reality in waiting.

FROM MY PERSONAL JOURNAL

REALITY

D_{o...} A_{lign...} **R**eality... E_{xpectations}

WHAT IS YOUR REALITY? Are you sure it is yours? Are you living by your design—or someone else's?

Your reality is what you choose it to be. Your world can be one of opportunity and unlimited possibilities. It can be full of scary corners and dark shadows. You get to choose.

Believe your BIG DREAM will come true, and it will become your reality.

How can I make such a bold statement? Are there not certain givens in this world? Aren't millions of people living in devastating circumstances? Aren't the systems that used to frame our world—economic, governmental and otherwise—breaking down? Aren't uncertainty, fear and dissatisfaction at an all-time high?

Collectively, we as citizens of this planet are living in a time when change seems to be everywhere...and happening at record speed. Why then are some people optimistic and thriving, while others are building underground bunkers? Same set of circumstances; totally different responses. What determines a person's response to circumstances?

Responses are determined by a person's belief system. Each of us has developed our own belief system by lumping together what we have been taught and what we have experienced. Psychologists refer to this as conditioning. As we go through life, we weave together an intricate system of conscious and unconscious beliefs that determine how we will respond to what happens to us and around us.

This is very good news . . . because you have the power to change your beliefs and your conditioned responses at any time.

All you have to do is become aware of the beliefs you have, take a good look at them, determine if they serve you, and change them if they don't. You are not a tree. You do not have to stay put and grow where you are planted.

In a nutshell, if you don't like your life, just change your beliefs.

I know this sounds very simplistic. In fact, you might be a bit put off right now. But stick with me for a minute.

Your beliefs are the foundation on which everything you do will stand. You need to make sure that your foundation is solid and built from materials that will support what you want to build on top of it.

If you are not sure what your beliefs are, just take a look at your current circumstances. Your current reality is a direct reflection of your current beliefs.

Beliefs are sneaky little creatures. We live by them even when we don't know they are there. Beliefs are also creatures of habit. Because beliefs are habits—let's call them habitual thinking patterns—like any habit, they can be changed. You just need to focus on a new thinking pattern, and practice it. Over a short period of time (usually 21 days or less), you will form a new thinking pattern and your new belief will replace your old belief.

If you are willing to look your current beliefs straight in the eye, you can determine if they are serving you and where your passion and purpose are leading you. If a belief is holding you back or limiting you, replace it with one that reflects who you are becoming as you move forward—and closer to your dreams.

Certainly seems worth the effort, doesn't it.

The only thing that stands between you and your dreams is your beliefs. This is very good news. You have the power to change your beliefs at any time. The power to attain your dreams rests in your hands, your heart, and your belief in YOURSELF. Your beliefs will always determine your reality. You are in charge of what you believe. Therefore, you have the power to shape your reality into your most passionate desire.

FROM MY PERSONAL JOURNAL

Matt is a salesman trying to prove himself in a very competitive world. As part of his job, he is required to use cold calling to build up a sales pipeline.

Somewhere during his career, he developed this belief: "If first thing in the morning I get ten rejections in a row, it means I am going to have a bad day and not make any sales."

Every day, as he makes his calls and gets closer and closer to the dreaded 10th rejection threshold, he becomes apprehensive. He wonders if the tenth rejection will "prove" that he is going to have a bad day.

As he continues to make calls, he begins to feel fearful. The apprehension he feels creeps into his voice. He starts thinking about his bad day rather than listening to the customer.

His apprehension virtually guarantees that he will get the ominous tenth rejection. When he does, his emotional state, which is already low, plummets.

Matt is now absolutely sure he is going to have a bad day. His despair makes him even less effective. After a few hours, he stops cold calling all together. He has proven his belief.

The next day he starts the process all over again, haunted by his tenth rejection superstition.

Matt has developed a belief that creates a spiral of future failure.

If you are going to doubt
anything, doubt your limits.

FROM MY PERSONAL JOURNAL

EXPECTATIONS

D₀... Aₗᵢₘₙ... Rₑₐₗᵢₜᵧ... Expectations

WHAT DO YOU EXPECT from life? What do you expect from and for yourself? What do you expect from your BIG DREAM?

The answers to the questions above will determine what you get. "Cause and effect" is a universal law. So is "expect and get."

On the previous page, we met Matt. He has developed a belief based on some arbitrary benchmark that has the power to make his day good or bad. He *expects* to have a bad day if he gets ten cold call rejections in a row at the beginning of his day. This affects his performance. This feeds his belief. Matt is caught in a self- defeating downward spiral. He has begun to expect "failure," so that is what he gets.

I feel for Matt. I feel for all of us who, at one time or another, have taken on a belief that keeps what we want just outside of our grasp. It is a frustrating and awful feeling. To save ourselves from that frustration, we lower our expectations so that, maybe, we won't be disappointed. Sometimes people just stop in their tracks and they never switch trains and go down another more positive path.

If Matt was sitting in front of me right now, this is what I would tell him.

"You have given your power to succeed away to something outside of yourself. I want you to take it back. And you **can** take it back. For today, expect good things! Tomorrow, expect good things, again! And see what happens. You can do this. I believe in you."

There are times when it is positive for us to pause, regroup and start with the basics. One of the most basic things we can do is **EXPECT GREAT THINGS**.

I trust that when Matt, and you, begin to expect good things, more good things will show up in your lives. That is how things work. By exercising your personal power and directing your will, you can focus your attention on those good things as they show up. Celebrate them! This creates the experience of expecting and getting good things. Soon, your life becomes a positive upward spiral.

Then, expect even more good things. You'll begin to like the feeling so much, you'll be soaring before you know it!

Double Dare:

a challenge that is

harder or naughtier

than a regular dare.

WEBSTER'S

When you get older, it's not what you did that you regret. It's what you didn't do.

GRACE SLICK

I DOUBLE DARE YOU

HAVE ALREADY DARED YOU to Dream Big. And we have gone through an exploration to see if you are willing to

D O
what it takes to

A LIGN
your

R EALITY
with your

E XPECTATIONS

But this dare is so important, I want to take it one step further.

Actually going for and living your BIG DREAM is so important to you, to everyone whose life you touch and the world,

It deserves a DOUBLE DARE.

So…..

I DOUBLE DARE YOU!!

Why Wait!

You actually have the power
to change your life today.

Right now.

Without thinking anymore about it.

All you have to do is

Take the DARE!

Come on.

You and your dreams are worth it...

Behind every success,

there lies a magical

word: Dare!

MEHMET MURANT ILDAN

Taking the DREAM BIG DARE is
not a matter of life and death.

It is a matter of life and LIFE.

You deserve a big, fully-lived LIFE!

FROM MY PERSONAL JOURNAL

TAKING THE DARE

BE FOREWARNED.
When you take the DREAM BIG DARE, your life will change immediately. The moment you take the dare, you become a magnet for things that will assist you in making your dream a reality. And what you have been longing for will have moved one giant step closer to you.

Be ready. Keep your eyes open. Look around. Expect miracles.

When you take the dare, here are a few simple things that will help keep you on track.

1 Always keep your focus on your BIG DREAM.

2 Write your BIG DREAM on five 3 x 5 cards and carry one with you at all times. Place the other four where you can see them throughout your day. Make changes as needed to keep you inspired. (Always BIGGER!)

3 Say "Yes" to things that show up that support your dream.

4 Say "No, thank you. Not now," to those things that do not support your dream. Move on.

5 Put together a support system of encouragers that believe in you and your right to have your dream become your reality.

6 Keep the faith.

That's all it takes. Write these guidelines on post it notes and stick them up all over the place. Write them on notecards and stick them in your wallet, in your pockets, in your drawers, inside the refrigerator . . . you get the idea. Write them on your calendar pages. Be willing to do what it takes to keep your BIG DREAM and these simple support ideas in front of you.

You are on your way!

The Power of Commitment

"Until one is committed

there is hesitancy, the
chance to draw back,

always ineffectiveness.

Concerning all acts of
initiative (and creation),

there is one elementary truth,

the ignorance of which
kills countless ideas

and splendid plans:

That the moment one definitely
commits oneself,

then Providence moves too.

All sorts of things occur to help one

that would never otherwise
have occurred.

A whole stream of events
issues from that decision,

raising in one's favor all manner

of unforeseen incidents and meetings
and material assistance,

which no man could have dreamt
would come his way."

W.M. MURRAY
(on the first American Expedition to reach the summit
of Mount Everest, led by Sir William McKinley).

You don't have to be great to get started,
but you have to get started to be great.

LES BROWN

ARE YOU IN?

ULTIMATELY IT IS YOU that chooses what your dreams are worth. It is up to you. Just you.

I can tell you that you are big enough, good enough, strong enough, deserving enough, skilled enough, determined enough, blessed enough, and important enough to have every single one of your dreams come true.

You have to believe it. You have to be willing to step up, trust and go for it.

So. Are you in?

Say yes and make this one of the best days of your life!

Now, pat yourself on the back. Call your best friends and tell them. Tell your partner and your kids. Heck, tell your cat or dog. Email me at **DreamBig@ThePalmieriGroup.com** and tell me! (I have a BIG SURPRISE waiting for you when I get your email.)

**Get a big piece of paper and
write on it in thick marker,**

"I just took the DREAM BIG DARE!!!"

Now Celebrate!

You have just bet on yourself.

And that is one bet you will always win!

Way to go!!!

Every great dream begins with a dreamer. Always remember, you have within you the strength, the patience, and the passion to reach for the stars to change the world.

HARRIETT TUBMAN

Time to Check In

**Before you go on to the last
chapter, check in with yourself.**

To have your BIG DREAM become a reality, you
must participate. Believing in it is not enough.
Wanting it is not enough. **You have to show up
and participate.**

The exercises in this book are a way you
can participate, right now, in making your BIG
DREAM your reality.

Think about the following questions so that you can gather some useful information. There are no right or wrong answers. No one will read your answers. They are between you and You.

- Did you do the exercises?
    ❏ YES   ❏ NO

- Did you spend time digging into the questions and learning from them? If not, Why?

_____

_____

_____

_____

_____

If you have not yet worked through the exercises and questions, go back and do them now.

Every time you practice participating, it becomes more natural to you and your inspired action muscle gets stronger and stronger.

Give full-out participation a shot. Invest a few more minutes and some elbow grease! I guarantee you will feel great, have a deeper connection with your BIG DREAM and be further ahead on the path to living it!

Develop an attitude of gratitude, and give thanks for everything that happens to you, knowing that every step forward is a step toward achieving something bigger and better than your current situation.

BRIAN TRACY

YOUR FIRST GOLDEN KEY

Gratitude

ON YOUR JOURNEY TO your BIG DREAM, you will discover keys that will keep you inspired and moving forward.

As my gift to you for embarking on this journey, I would like to share with you a Golden Key that has made a bigger difference in my life than all the other keys I have discovered.

That key is Gratitude.

Gratitude is the most powerful emotion on earth. It is universal. It is pure when given from the heart. And it is the ultimate way to keep you aligned with your passion, purpose, vision and your BIG DREAM.

The best way to have more of what you want is to be grateful for what you have.

So, here is your first Golden Key. Use it with my blessings and my best wishes.

Let's Make It Real

The best way to use your first Golden Key is to be grateful right here, right now.

Just read the statement below and fill in the blank.

"I am so happy and grateful now that . . .

_____

_____

_____

_____

_____

_____

By being willing to take the DREAM BIG DARE, you have guaranteed that you will have more of what you want in your life. Your willingness to DREAM BIG, and do something about it, serves not only you, but ALL OF US.

Something I am grateful for today is YOU and your BIG DREAM!

Go for it!
Enjoy the journey.

Never give up on what you really want to do. The person with big dreams is more powerful than one with all the facts.

ALBERT EINSTEIN

ACKNOWLEDGEMENTS

WHENEVER I WOULD MENTION to someone I was writing a book, people would often ask who was helping me. While I did not have a co-author, that question was tough to answer because this book would have never have reached your hands without countless people's help. This book came at a time of great personal transformation. I am blessed and guided by many inspiring spirits who unknowingly contributed to this book.

First, I want to thank my wife, life partner and muse, Carolyn. She listened to me for years about someday writing a book and continued to encourage me when I found other things to do. Her constant words of it's time for you to share with the world your passion and belief that all people can be what they want to be and start living their dream. She shows me the door marked "Roger's Time." With her unfailing strength I finally made the detour from my door of security and passionately opened the door to my inspiration. She is always my tireless champion.

Second, my dear friend, Todd Courtney. We met over 24 years ago when he attended one of my public seminars. We became friends and just over a year ago he called to get together for a beer and catch up. When we met on that Friday afternoon, he said, "So how's that book comin' along?" I said, "What book?", and he said, "You know, that book that you're supposed to write." Todd went on to say, "It's your time and the world needs your Dream Big book."

To Steve Murnin, another great and valued friend for more than twenty years. The "big thinker" who continues to encourage and support me in all my teaching and training endeavors.

To Karen Stone, MSW, LCC, contributor, who provided valuable insights and perspectives to my material. I am immensely grateful for her ability to pull this book together after countless interviews and the barrage of my writings. Her amazing skills at integrating, editing, and synthesizing information are responsible for the clarity of this book.

Third, my friend, Bob Bare, a terrific advisor, friend, and founder of BestSellingExperts.com. His practical advice has been indispensable.

To Joel Osteen, Pastor of Lakewood Church, my constant reminder of excellence and integrity, who has continued to inspire and encourage me to stay on my spiritual path.

A few more people deserve a special recognition for their invaluable contribution:

Don Jessup   Larry Tringali
LeFrancis Arnold   John Finnegan
Edith Espinola   Anne Hernandez
Peter Yee   Greg Grialou
Adrianne Castillo   Sam Oceguera
Jacqueline Courtney   Dora Calantog
Jim Myrick   Dan Pantoja

Thanks to all the students and attendees of my classes, lectures and seminars over the years who contributed to this book coming to fruition.

ABOUT ROGER AND
HIS BIG DREAM

I BELIEVE STRUGGLE AND LIFE circumstances are given to each of us to show us what we are really made of inside. Each obstacle is an opportunity to discover the depth of who we are and who we consciously chose to be. My life path has shown me, without a doubt, that we each have the ability to make our life into what we want it to be. In fact, it became my life mission to learn to do this for myself. Then it became my passion to share what I have learned and to be a guide and an example to others who want to make significant lasting changes in their lives. This passion drives my life.

Of course, I did not know these things until later in my life. First I had to learn to rise above obstacles. I had to reach a low point in my emotional struggles before I was open to receiving the gift of divine intervention. And I had to search, study, experiment and go through good ole' trial and error.

My obstacles began very early in my life. My parents divorced when I was only two years old and I became the rope in their emotional tug of war. I felt that I was not wanted or loved and that I did not belong. Luckily, my grandmother, aunt and uncle showed me love and gave me some sense of belonging. Yet I began seeking for another group where I felt at home. When I was 12, a neighbor of mine introduced me to a group of surfers, and I experienced true belonging for the first time. I was tan and happy until I graduated from high school.

I "came of age" during the height of the Vietnam War. Feeling a patriotic obligation to serve my country, I enlisted in the Marine Corps where I would meet my best friend Dave. We were deployed to Vietnam. Twenty-three days later, he was killed right in front of my eyes in a fire fight. I was overwhelmed with grief, sadness and anger and became a changed man as I lived through the horrors of war.

When I returned to the US, I had no direction or purpose, and was plagued with depression and all-encompassing rage. More than ever I needed family. However, nothing had changed. I tried self-medicating to ease the emotional pain. Nothing worked. Then one Thursday afternoon, I took my hopelessness, anger, pain, and disillusionment to a pew in a quiet church. I got on my knees and prayed. After a while, a feeling of peacefulness came over me. I lifted myself from my knees and sat in the pew. I noticed a crumpled piece of paper next to me, picked it up and opened it. Scribbled on it were these words: "If it's meant to be, it's up to me."

That moment changed my life. I decided then and there to do whatever it takes to live a purposeful life and to make a positive difference.

My first project was myself. I wanted to change and improve my attitudes and habits. I began talking to others about my new found direction, and realized I was not alone—many people wanted to create lasting positive change in their lives, but didn't know how. I became hungry to find out how people, including me, could improve their lives. I enrolled in college and began taking evening psychology classes while I worked during the day. Always an avid reader (I began reading the Encyclopedia Britannica at age 7), I studied psychology, philosophy, how our minds work, and the writings of great teachers throughout history, Aristotle, Plato, Socrates, Jesus, Buddha, and including current teachers such as Earl Nightingale, Napolean Hill, Og Mandino, Zig Ziglar, Jim Rohn, Bob Proctor, Buckminister Fuller, Doug Edwards, Cavett Robert, Werner Erhard, B.F. Skinner, and many, many others.

As I studied and practiced what I was learning, I started creating my life by design rather than by chance. People began to notice. They wanted to know what I was doing, and I shared my ideas and experiences. They suggested I share this information with as many people as I could.

That was over 35 years ago. I stood up, looked myself in the eyes, felt my heart beating, and dared to step up and create a life worth living. My dreams began to come true. They still are. Over the years, my BIG DREAM has gotten bigger and bigger. I am still learning, growing and sharing. I stay focused on being the best I can be and serving others to the best of my ability. And my Big Dreams keep coming true. Every day, for this, I am extremely grateful.

Roger lives with the love of his life, his wife Carolyn, and their two dogs, Louie and Gina, in San Jose, California. He is an internationally sought after speaker, seminar/ workshop leader and Mind-Set Performance Expert Coach.

For more information about Roger and his products and workshops, please visit www.ThePalmieriGroup.com or email him at DreamBig@ThePalmieriGroup.com.

66 Pursue what
you are
passionate about—
That's how dreams
come true. 99

ROGER PALMIERI

RESOURCES

Roger's CD Program:

Dream Big

I Dare You ... Better Yet .... I Double Dare You

- 6 CD's Learning System for Behavior Modification utilizing a proven and tested Mind-Set Neuro Training System.

- A Powerful Life Changing Program That Will Inspire You With Breakthrough Methods To Boost Performance, Profits, Productivity and People.

For more information on
Roger's keynote and
breakout speaking events
for your company or
organization contact him at
DREAMBIG@ThePalmieriGroup.com
or call (408) 658-8161.

For additional information
regarding Roger's programs
and materials please visit
www.ThePalmieriGroup.com.

SPECIAL SALES

This book is available at
special quantity discounts when
purchased in bulk by companies,
corporations, organizations, and
special interest groups.

For information, please email
DREAMBIG@ThePalmieriGroup.com
or call (408) 658-8161

CPSIA information can be obtained at www.ICGtesting.com
Printed in the USA
LVOW10*2059150514

385955LV00012B/385/P